LOW TIDE

M.

Typeset and Published
by
The National Poetry Foundation
(Reg Charity No 283032)
27 Mill Road
Fareham
Hants PO16 0TH
(Tel: 01329 822218)

Printed by
Meon Valley Printers
Bishops Waltham (01489 895460)

Sponsored by Rosemary Arthur

Cover photograph by Celia Rambaut

Edited by Johnathon Clifford

Poetry previously published in *Chester Poets Anthology XVII* and *Pause 42*.

ISBN 1 870556 49 6

CONTENTS

For Jenny Tweedie, WEA tutor,
who challenged me to try poetry

and

Gladys Mary Coles
who shared her knowledge
and her know-how.

WHITE PEAK SPRING

Between Ilam, Youlgreave and Alstonefield
High pasture lies, a billowing quilt
White-sewn with dry-stone walls.

Over Thorpe Cloud, Arbor Low, Parsley Hey,
Lark-song cascades over calling lambs
To staccato mock of cuckoo.

Through Dovedale and Lathkill Dale
Running bass of ribbling river,
Trout in rock pools, wagtails, dippers.

In Hartington and Tissington
Gilley-flowers spatter lime-grey houses,
Petals reflect old stories at the wells.

By Mill Dale and Miller's Dale
Cliffs and crags grow bluebells underfoot,
Yellow catkins curtain caves.

Between Buxton, Ashbourne and Matlock Bath
High pasture lies a billowing quilt
White-sewn with dry-stone walls.

TWO PICTURES
(*Walker Art Gallery, Liverpool*)

Selling Chickens in Liguria by Henry la Tangue

Sophie tucks a protesting cockerel
Under each arm;
Curling plumes flash bronze,
Scarlet combs quiver indignation.
She darts a black-eyed glance back
At Peppi, trying his luck with the screeching cart
At the mayor's door.
A cheeky one that, with his red bandana
Worn like a bandit.
The ochre cobbles burn her bare soles -
Thin, oval stones laid on edge
Like stacks of unleavened bread in the bakers -
They pattern the sunlit street;
The soft folds of Sophie's creamy dress,
Catching the bright light,
Mirror the same design.
Leaf shadows mottle the amber walls.
It is almost siesta
And half the chickens still to sell.

A Street In Brittany by Stanhope Forbes

A clomp of sabots brings Francine to the door,
Fingers busy with fleece and spindle.
Her shy glance along the narrow street
Cheers her, the square stones lemon
In the Spring light.
Neighbours are out enjoying the pale sun;
Salt-white aprons flap
Against the cobalt shade.
The women tease her gently,
Secretly envy her fair skin,
Blonde hair under the snowy cap,
Eyes washed blue as her stiff peasant skirt,
The demure half-smile.

THE DEED BOX

Old Fred, retiring secretary,
Asked me to keep it safe:
A rusty old tin box
Stuffed with letters,
Minute books, newspaper cuttings,
Cards and records of the fishing club
Since its inception a century ago.

Hours I spent that Winter,
Cosy by the burbling fire,
Delving, sifting, sorting . . .
Out of those fading scraps
A sepia newsreel flickered:

Inaugural meeting, Hotel Imperial,
Chaired by a Major of waxed moustaches,
Gold albert winking behind his whiskey glass;

A Bank Holiday waggonette,
Crowded with committee men
Off to explore the woods and farms
In search of fishing waters;
A map from nineteen hundred and three
Charting the many pools they found and rented;
A yellowing copper-plate invoice
For three hundred perch from Windermere
To stock the waters.

'Fisherman's Tickets' at six pence
For the Railway outing to Chirk,
Members humping rods and baskets
Miles to catch the early train;

A list of the catch
At the Spring competition
In nineteen hundred and six.
Pike, Perch, Rudd, Roach,
Carp, Bream, and Tench.

A detailed account of the Smoking Concert
Carefully cut from the local *Reporter*;
Pipes and tobacco the gift of His Lordship.
Toasts flowing fast as big fish stories.
Primed with punch provided by the Patron.

Now, when I sit by a tree-fringed pond
Catching across the fields
The ebb and flow of church bells on the wind,
I have these shady companions,
Wielding Bohemian greenheart rods,
Flicking the plaited flax as skilfully
As I manage my nylon filament.

THE SHOP

Grandfather started the firm;
Astute, austere, wing collar stiff.
Ramrod back, bristle moustache,
Homburg. He never wasted words
Or anything else. Saved assiduously
And began 'Kay's Hatters & Hosiers'.
Rented a good position
On Stamford Street with
Plenty of passing trade,
Half of it clothing cheques.
The shop was open till eight at night
Or later, when the last loiterer
Chose to leave. His stock
Was tunic shirts, separate collars,
Flat caps, trilbies, socks and ties,
Uniform roundel caps
For Ashton and Manchester Grammar.

Grandfather chose our coats and suits
Wholesale from the warehouse;
Always two sizes too large
And way out of fashion:
"You'll grow into it. Good cloth that.
Last you for years."

Upstairs was used for stock
But the window gave a grandstand view
Of the Black Knight Pageant;
Sir Ralph de Assheton astride
A sable hunter, armour gleaming
Darkly like the kitchen range:
Sinister as his wicked deeds,
Rolling defaulters down-hill
In a barrel full of spikes
They used to say.
Grandfather said
"It was no good for trade."

Nor the Whit Walks,
Brass blaring, banners high,
Crowds ogling the faithful,
Witnessing in sober pomp
And new Whissunday[1] splendour;
"Empty show, empty show!
All in pawn by Monday -
No customers for hours."

[1]*Spelt as pronounced in parts of Lancashire.*

"HE'S IN HIS ROOM"

Whenever he is wounded
He retreats to his strong-hold
Sets up his defences against interrogation
Pulls up the drawbridge,
Cuts all lines of communication.

In vain I keep patient siege
Sending my carrier pigeons
With tempting messages, offering
Food-aid or an ally's strength,
Attempt a diplomatic mission.

All I receive in reply
Is boiling oil of rejection,
Arrows dispatch my counsel
Until I withdraw, defeated

To nurse my own wound,
Cope with my impotence.
He is a warrior now,
Scorning the soft bosoms of camp-followers,
Even his mother's.

PASSPORT

I can never think of Les
Without that head-hugging black beret
Its patina of engine oil
Rusted by smears of old red lead,
The Tranmers burgee tarnished with salt,
Whisps of ginger escaping from the leather band.

It was his proud badge of office
And passport to the family circle.
He was Dad's first mate,
Chief engineer and everlasting side-kick.
His small face and cheery repartee were
Part of Sunday tea week in week out
When their sailing summer was over,
A baffle to Father's endless spiel
On cars, cameras, craft, records and radio.

He outlived his skipper by thirty years.
If it had been the other way,
Dad would have draped his coffin
With the tatty red duster
Faded by salt spray and exhaust fumes
And placed the ancient beret on the top.

AUGUST '39

Tanned eager faces
Circled the holiday table
Anticipating
A new breakfast experience:

In turn we poured the creamy milk
Over the feather-light bubbles
Of pale puffed grain;
Each bent an attentive ear
To the snap crackle and pop.

Chuckles, wide smiles, chinking spoons.

Father bent his ear
To the crackling radio
Concentrating on clipped, cold news:

"Pack up Mother, we're going home!"
Eyes popped,
Grins snapped,
Spoons stopped;
A whole week before term began!

The wicker-work skip crackled
Crammed with buckets, spades and bathing suits,
Shorts, sand shoes, sailing smocks.

Sardined inside the old Daimler
We waved goodbye to our chalet,
Promising, next year, to return.

We never did go back.

LAMENT

In those days the evening street
Was loud and lively;
Shrieks of girls criss-crossed
In games of tag,
'Barley' and 'Rally-o'
Ricocheted down the road,
Posses galloped by snap-snapping cap-guns,
A ragged-seated lad
Swung round-a-bout from a lamppost,
Miniature mums paraded tiny prams,
Clacketing heisted high heels,
Robin Hood ambushed from an alley way,
Battered bicycles skidded
Dirt-track circles
Outside the corner shop.

Now when I stand at the door
On a Summer evening,
Silent motor cars crouch along the kurb,
No children play.
From every curtained window
The Pied Piper's music blares,
Where his magic lantern mesmerises
With flickering pictures in the dark.

MIGRANT SPIDERS

The meadow is soft gossamer
Shimmering in morning sun:
A thousand invisible vagrants
Have been wandering.
Hitching a lift on the breeze
Each careless vagabond taking the air,
And going - anywhere -
A minute mariner
Ever adventuring his limitless Pacific,
His only Kon-Tiki a silken thread.

MEXICANS

Grandmother, daughter and child,
Black hair glistening,
A proud and statuesque trio
Wrapped in blankets
Of bold geometry; sun colours
Spun and woven
By themselves, for sale:
A people holding fast
To their own.

A blind potter
By her pot-bellied vase,
Terra-cotta glazed with black design;
Blind eyes seeing through her
Loneliness and penury
To fierce independence.

The Pueblo with his wooden saints,
The figures thick, the carving crude,
But his face - nut brown -
Contoured with a thousand lines
As a map of mountain country;
A mouth firmed by toil
In a long peasant life,
The far-seeing gaze of the desert-dweller,
Patiently accepting.

PARADISE LOST

It was a mistake to come back,
To expect the place to be the same.
The shop which used to be
Aladdin's cave,
Is small-town-seedy,
The beach has shrunk,
Golden sands paled
To dirty Horlicks,
Spume at the tide's edge
A creamy scum.
A bitter wind hurls litter
Into the corner
Where we wriggled
Into woollen bathing suits.
Thump and clang of machinery
Interferes from across the estuary.
Hoping to regain paradise
I find only a microcosm
Of today's degradation.

LOW TIDE, CULLEN[1]

Below the harbour's steep stone sides
A gleaming expanse of mud,
Gravelled with pebbles,
Each with its shadow-arc

Empty
But for one small boy,
Feet planted in ooze,
Long shadow before him.
Still as an old groyne stump
With a bubbly crown of weed.
Gazing seaward,
Dreaming,
Longing for his Dad to bring the fish,
Trailing his raucous cloud of gulls
When the grey water covers the shore again.

[1]*A small fishing village on the Scottish East Coast.*

CAPE GOOSEBERRIES

I remember in the Donegal cottage
How we enjoyed feeding the fire
From the huge basket of turves.
How we curled on the soft sofa
Sharing the puzzle in the paper
By the quiet glow of the peat.

I remember the fire in the old house;
The hot coals red, falling, flaming,
Reflecting in the beaten-copper scuttle.
How a sudden hiss and flare
Lifted eyes from books, prompted the placing
Of a shining black cob into the fierce heart.

I remember long weeks of confinement;
The luxury of a fire in the bedroom
Crackling and leaping in the dark,
Huge fantastic shadows overhead,
Sibilant sighing of the steam-kettle,
The wrap-around warmth of home.

My son's house has no fire-place.
The heating is insidious,
Remote-controlled.
The focal point is a plastic gadget
Flickering never-ending technicolour
And incessant noise.

His wife has arranged Cape Gooseberries
In a vase; tangerine tissue lanterns
Complementing green furnishings.
The cheerful, vibrant seed-cases
Masquerading like a cold postcard
From a sun-drenched holiday.

BEACH-COMBING

1.

These dry bubbles of cellulose
Rasping the palm of my hand
Once washed in the ocean,
Were moist, flesh-filled,
Pregnant with specks of life,
As a cluster of grapes
On a warm terrace
Plump, ripen and fall
To yield the black seeds.

2.

This whorled and pointed skeleton
With pearly hollow,
Home of a lost sea-creature,
Incessant restless waves
Will tumble, wear and pound
Against rocks, pebbles, ground
Until it shatters, scatters,
Pulverised to grains of sand
With opalescent specks that glisten
Like jewel dust in the sun.
Then children's feet will run
Over the gritty surface,
Small hands dig and pat the gold
Into fantastic castles.

ULLSWATER WASHING DAY

A drying wind, fresh as bleached sheets:
Aira[1] tumbles her washing-water
from a great height,
it thunders white
through the narrow flume,
spills roaring into the cauldron -
sock-water swirling soapy suds.

Over the village
a pale cloud spills
a bucketful of rain.
Beams of silver sunlight
slant on a waterside farm,
creaming flapping towels,
burnishing bracken.

By the lake
trees stand shoulder to shoulder,
long warrior shields,
gold, bronze, brass, copper,
counterpoint of dark green.

Beyond, mountains,
dark as plum pudding portions,
silver sixpences
peeping from the sides,
brandy sauce pouring down.

[1]*'Aira Force' is a waterfall which empties into Ullswater*

THE MAGDALEN
(From a painting by Paulus Bor in the Walker Gallery)

Well, I've done it!
Spent every last farthing.
I've never held anything so precious.
I'm terrified I'll drop it.
See Thomas frown at me.
He suspects I've stolen it, no doubt.

It seemed like a wonderful idea at the time.
But how will they see it?
Call me a silly show-off?
Judas will complain about the cost.
They don't think much of me.
But he . . .

Well they don't show him
Much appreciation;
Falling out amongst themselves,
Wanting to be top of the table.
Someone has to show him,
Like Samuel annointed David.

He poured love over me.
He didn't look askance
As if I'd crawled out
From under the carpet.
What does it matter
What they think!

AFTER THE FUNERAL
(A memory of my father)

I peered into the garage
through a cobwebbed window:
there was his lathe
below the murky pane,
still fuzzy with shavings.

I could smell hot lubricant,
see him standing there
in his 'ratting jacket'
among the paraphernalia
of his precious Sundays -
oil can, tool rack,
off-cuts of steel and brass,
cleaning rags -

grubby fingers fondling
his latest artifact -
a cigarette lighter
inlaid with burnished pennies.

These were his weekend joys,
shrugging off the company director
with the pin-stripe suit.
In tatty jersey and flannels
he was a truant school-boy
escaping to the woods.

MONDAY

You could always tell it was washing day
Before you reached the back-yard gate,
Billows of bleachy steam would meet you
Carrying the squeal of the turning mangle.
Nellie stood sturdy on bandy legs
Beside the stubborn iron machine
As one hand turned and turned the handle
The other grasped the hot wet shirt
And fed it through the wooden rollers.

Pale lips in the lined face pressed in effort
Again the flaccid arm dipped in the tub
And thrust long-johns and petticoats
Bodices and tablecloths, sheets and handkerchieves
Through the greedy squeezer.
The fat ribbed aluminium tub
Frothed up its last into the wicker basket.
Straightening painfully she breathed
"That's two lots done!"

The first lot clap-flapped on the line.
Gas hissed under the ancient boiler
Whiff of stew wafted from the kitchen.
Thin mouth widened in a satisfied smile,
"This is better than working in t'mill."
Feeling for the hem of her wrap-around apron
She lifted it to wipe her dripping nose,
Tucked white whisps of hair into her cap,
Dipped the blue bag into rinsing water.

Humming to herself a musical hall song
She stirred the starch into a bowl
Then gripping hard the rubbing board,
Tackled a tub full of nappies:
Slap, press, drumma-drum, slap, press, drumma-drum,
Swollen knuckles bulging white
Banishing stains with jaw set tight.
"Grand wash day!" Shouts father coming home,
"Champion! I'll 'ave yer dinner out directly!"

ODIOUS COMPARISON

I spent a morning marvelling
At the tiger's glowing coat,
The peacock's shimmer,
Shy grace of the gazelle
And somnolence of lions.

At lunchtime in the café
Homo Sapiens disappoints:
A grey coach driver
Chain smoking in my face,
An uncouth youth in
Tatty jeans and T-shirt,
Two shapeless grannies scoffing cakes,
Their pink scalps peeping
Through fuzz of thinning hair.
Three male blobs, beer bellies bulging
Guzzle egg and chips and sloppy tea.
A stout mother
Squeezed into jogging suit,
Slaps at snuffly children
Whining for ice-cream.

Pocketing my sandwiches
I sneak out of the door:
Sharing with the pigeons in the sun
I watch the sea-lions dive and play
Their feeding time away.

THE YACHT CLUB, ROCK PARK

Dilapidated now, prostituted,
the Georgian mansion standing four square
above the river in the once exclusive park.

In the lofty first floor drawing room
the spirit of the old sea captain gazes
mournfully over the empty river.

The ghost of his lady regards
the patch of neglected lawn below;
all that remains of her splendid garden
is the Japanese tree, bare
wrinkled and twisted, with weeping downward fingers.

She looks sourly askance at the rough men
in faded jeans and dusty woollen hats
working where her flowers once grew,
drinking beer beside their upturned dinghies
and battered sailing craft.

But her husband drifts happily among these latter days,
signalling their heady perfume of varnish,
gristling away with sandpaper.
He understands their longing, their imagining,
their flight from office desks,
from cramping wife and kids.

The faraway look in the yachtsmen's eyes
is reflected in his own.

SICK BAY

Figures swim on the page, thoughts flicker
uncatchable as bats,
head thumps, throat aches.

Exiled to dim-lit dark
I stagger to strange bed,
tossing through night-sweats,
pain and fitful fears
of starched and tight-lipped matron.

Apron rustles thin daylight,
kind cold of soothing cloth,
quenching orange juice and
soft jelly to slide down stinging throat.

Propped in soft pillows
I survey the room of empty beds:
mercifully muted covers of midnight blue
striped with white sheets,
walls of delicate palest green
fresh as a shower;
a picture opposite, like a large window
onto a simple slope of hillside
covered in blowing meadow grass,
daisies, cowslip, lady's smock.

Drench for hot eyes,
washing away fear and fever.

Wood pigeons' throaty matins
rouse me. Subdued and desultory
the singing of other birds.

I ease the window wide
and breathe moist air.
Dark lines define the hills
against the mist.
Soft cloud covers Helm Crag.
The garden is a monotone palette
of dark conifers,
lime-fresh deciduous trees,
smooth lawns steamy and still.

By me a pink rose lazily sways
against grey-green slabs of slate.

Will it be a day of warm drizzle
or will the strong sun
burn it all away
to leave us scorching?

WINTER

He strode away
over the marshes,
his shadow-form diminishing
in dank winter mist
until he was as lost as the farther shore.

Leaving her
in flat emptiness
with only the blanched grasses,
bent bleached reeds,
glinting water smudged with sooty wild fowl

and lonely grey sheep
motionless as boulders.

ABBEY SQUARE

Early morning lightens the bishop's garden,
cold lowering clouds cover November sky.
Beneath, the slanting shafts of early sun
warm russet bricks and cream white window frames,
mellow red tiles and rusty gables, sculpting
the trees and tingeing them with gold. By noon
rain drums persistent on the pavement flags
polishing ancient cobbles in the square.
The leaves of the plane trees dance in the torrent,
from every gargoyle teems a gushing stream,
the cloister arches loom through misty veil
squalls spatter the lighted jewel glass,
black clerics billow across the close
and evensong organ warms the darkening day.

SPRING FEVER

Spring brings Mother out
in a rash of broom-fever;
top to bottom, inside out
the house is turned;
shelves and cupboards purged,
heavy mahogany furniture
shifted and cleaned behind,
every blanket washed and aired,
rugs hung out and thwacked
with wicker beater,
carpets spread on the lawn
unmercifully scrubbed.

Spring brings Father out
in virulent sea-fever:
every weekend happily busy
scraping barnacles, burning paint,
stuffing caulking into seams,
sanding-down, anti-fouling,
varnishing to mirror perfection.
Proofing sails, fettling stays,
reeving sheets through squealing blocks,
swinging the compass, checking the charts
and spending, spending, spending
at the Chandlers.

Spring brings me out
in a mood of deep dissatisfaction:
down from the attic, shaken and pressed,
come all last summer's dresses,
only to prove too small and shabby.
I tussle with scissors and needle,
unpick, make do,
until exasperation point.
Nothing will satisfy but something new
in the latest colour, fashion, size.
Shopping, I see every woman in town
has the same endemic fever.

DÉJÀ VU

One day in Quedlinburg
where timber-frame old houses
are caramel and chocolate
and sunlit cobbles lemon-drops,
I met a stranger
in Tyrolean jacket,
a feather in his hat.

His face was old and lean,
the hare-bell of his eyes
as lively as my children's were,
surprising in the swarthy skin.
Straw in a moonlit field
his hair appeared,
hiding long lobes
weighted by silver earrings.

I left him in the narrow street
but his dancing eyes and pointed face
stayed with me all the day:
certain I was I'd never met
so strange a man before, and yet,
something in my memory tugged.

Leafing through a battered book
of fairy tales that night
I found him, piping
along just such a street,
a smile about his lips
and all the children following.

RESERVATION

Yes, I would like to see the native crafts,
I would enjoy meeting the people
if I thought I could talk to them
plainly as equals
and they would see me so,

but to gawp at them
like curios in a museum,
to photograph
as if they were ancient sites,
flowers or trees, or at best
some willing extras
in a 'B' movie -

if I could see for real,
the copper braves, slender and lithe
riding their ponies after buffalo,
I would enjoy the chase,
sit afterwards in firelight
beside pointed tepees.
But I don't care to go
to see the government housing
and overweight, idle
hang-dog remnants
leaning at street corners
or propped at seedy bars.

Gerald used to say
we lived in a gold-fish bowl -
all the neighbours could see what we were doing.

Now he's gone
I think it more an advantage
to be at the top of the Close, at the T's centre.

Each Spring I watch
Irene's almond blossom open
and Richard's laburnum pour its yellow falls.

Summer brings lawns
neatly hemmed with flowers,
Impatiens, Lobelia and white Alysum.

Each morning early
the plumber revs his noisy diesel
loading it with copper pipes and cylinders.

Alan, with briefcase,
in Monday morning suit
drives off to the office in his big white Rover.

After the men have gone
Nancy limps over to Nell's
with a basket of breakfast and neighbourly concern.

Tess trundles off
trailing her shopping trolley,
waving back to Harry, shirt-sleeved at the gate.

The postman
weaves his way from house to house
and I hope today something will come for me,

for sometimes
my picture-window is just that -
a screen where unreal figures act out their busy lives.

Not touching mine.

OXFORD, NORTH CAROLINA

No dreaming spires here, no honeyed skyward Gothic
vague through the mist and smoke of an urban October,
but low white horizontals, clap-board houses, green lawns
and trees, trees - gold, crimson, scarlet, bronze.

Instead of college scarves and black gowns flying
in a chilling wind under a threatening grey,
Stars and Stripes and Hallowe'en banners flutter against blue,
along wide avenues where pedestrians are scarce.

There is no bustle and noise of students and shoppers,
bicycles, buses, squeezing through narrow streets;
Carolina folk drive their spacious roads at leisure,
visiting banks and diners in the comfort of their cars.

No vivacious shamble of market, shops and colleges,
where anoraks and cords, tweeds and jumpers jostle:
here farmers, stretching T-shirts over obesity
discuss tobacco sales and steers beside their pick-ups.

No lean ascetic faces poke into centuries of philosophy
oozing from ancient Cotswold stones endowed in medieval days.
History is callow here, the splendid library empty,
the only monument a lone Confederate soldier.

In England, Oxford's hems are rivers and watermeadows,
where ancient bridges carry you to rolling hills.
Its namesake is a patch among a forest wilderness,
sliced by two highways and a single railroad track.

Only a brash young town with a colonial Courthouse,
a few ostentatious neo-classical façades,
one Art Deco cinema and Baptist Chapels on every corner
could proudly call this small and sleepy place a city.

IN NORMANDY

Winding by deep lanes
through rolling fields,
frothing white orchards.

Meandering through old villages
of sunlit mellow stone,
sleeping cats and dogs.

Crossing an ancient bridge
over a broad slow-flowing river
glinting through reedy meadows.

Taking our *déjeuner sur l'herbe*
in cool shade by the water's edge
by basking red-brown cattle.

Watching the lazy curving eddies,
the trailing delicate willow boughs,
hovering dragonflies, droning bees.

Lingering in soporific bird song,
slow flap-flap of heron;
dozing, replete, lazy . . .

Screams stab awake . . ! Flesh creeps . . .
cacophony of frantic hens,
rising rooks, barking dogs.

Ominous silence . . . a rumbling cart,
slow, clopping donkey on the bridge,
old black peasant nodding.

Behind him couched in bloody straw
stiff, silent victim -
the slaughtered pig.

STATE FAIR

Park your Ford
where the State Trooper stands,
whistle in mouth and commanding hands,
by Chevvies, Pontiacs
and motor-caravans.

Follow your nose to hamburgers,
onions, charred chicken, french fries,
cajun fish, italian sausage.
See Percy Lee disappear
behind a cloud of cotton-candy.

Squeeze through crowds of obesity
bulging out of blue-jeans,
stuffing dead-pan faces -
chinese, hispanic, slav,
indian, negro, nordic.

Press on through bull bellow,
tractor roar and loud-speaker blare
to view the largest pig,
heftiest steer, Arabian stallion,
Percheron greys, Charolais.

Stay after dark for the razzamatazz
of lit carousels,
swaying swing-boat crescents,
the Ferris Wheel's diamond garland,
fireworks bustin' the night sky.

GARDEN

How many times I sat, grateful,
under your apple tree,
watching through shading lashes
the screen of branch and blossom,
deep Shropshire skies.

Leaving my frantic world,
how glad I was
to be again in your oasis
among the quiet hum of bees
and lazy noontide bird song,
drinking from you and the flowers
a soporific elixir melting my tension.

Even when my visits were to care for you
and set your chair beneath the apple tree,
we were sleek and quiet
as furry pussy willow basking.

Not even death,
lingering at your elbow,
could steal from us the calm.

WATCHING

It's great fun
watching rainbows skim the water,
sailboards leaping in the wind.

How dashing and powerful
the black figure
gripping the wishbone
pitting his strength
against the pull of the wind.

Will he stop in time,
can he turn?
The lake slowly swallows him,
his sail lies limp on the water.

It must be Christmas cold
but it's great fun watching.

Dinghies rock at the jetty,
tug painters, sails fuffling.

Gaggling the duckboards
behind the instructor,
like ducklings
come would-be sailors.

The first mainsail fills,
they're away!
But the jib still flaps.
Put it out goose-winged
on the other side!

They're going to hit that buoy,
up the helm!
They've got her in irons!

Put the rudder over,
lay off the wind,
let the sails fill!

It's terrible watching,
condemned to the leaden earth -
useless -
as the old salt in the picture,
spinning yarns for little boys.

TIME TRAVEL

A monotonous bell tolling
solemnly summoning
come, come
to tales of
inland seas and lonely sands,
mysterious magi caravans
and the heat of dusty cities
two thousand years away,

legends flying hope
far into an eternal future.

A plangent solitary sound
evoking a sea-bell tolling
a mournful warning,

memories' undertow
tugging to a shingle shore
where children caper
in Atlantic thunder,
antic Aphrodites
shining in the sun,

a shell-wrapped souvenir
of cliff crying sea gulls
where time has no existance
in a child's continual present.

PHYSICK

Pressed under platform paving stones
in a London railway station
lie the bones of Nicholas Culpeper.

Balm, Borage, Bergamot, Barbery.

Gone the apothecary's shop in Spitalfield
and buried in library reference rooms
his 'London Dispensatory'.

Cress, Coltsfoot, Caraway, Chamomile.

Tinctures and salves for healing wounds
and cooling draughts for child-bed fever,
strewing herbs, tisanes and tonics.

Lime, Lovage, Loose-strife, Liquorice.

The flowers which made his medicines still grow
in concrete cracks and pavement crevices
in graveyards and neglected gardens.

Mace, Mallow, Marjoram, Marigold.

Over three centuries of pounding feet,
the smoke and shake of heavy locomotives,
building and battle and rumbling traffic.

Rue, Rampion, Rosemary, Rattle-grass.

Gold and jewel colours illuminate
these dusty inhospitable streets,
like telling beads to sooth and sanctify.

Sage, Saffron, Savory, Sweet Cicely.

45

IN THE GENES

How like my mother's hands
my own have gone;

brown skin freckle-speckled
crisscross of tiny lines
veins wriggling like blue string
and knuckles too large
to slip the gold band off.

Those hands made countless apple-pies
bathed babies, beat carpets,
scrubbed floors, cleaned flues,
adminstered smacks and nasty medicine.
Bled, rubbing wet nappies.

These hands have led a lady's life.
Tapped keys, played tennis,
flicked a feather duster,
served coffee in delicate china cups
while machines gobbled the dirty work.

Yet, how like my mother's hands
my own have gone.